the
OTHER
SIDE of ME

the
OTHER
SIDE of ME

D O R O T H Y A N N E S U M M E R S

abbott press®
A DIVISION OF WRITER'S DIGEST

THE OTHER SIDE OF ME

Abbott Press books may be ordered through booksellers or by contacting:

Abbott Press
1663 Liberty Drive
Bloomington, IN 47403
www.abbottpress.com
Phone: 1-866-697-5310

ISBN: 978-1-4582-0740-1 (sc)
ISBN: 978-1-4582-0739-5 (e)

Library of Congress Control Number: 2012923528

Printed in the United States of America

Abbott Press rev. date: 2/13/2013

To
Dorothy Anne
With Love
Aunt Dorothy

Acknowledgements

First, to my husband, Ralph
For encouraging me to have these poems published.

My daughter, Sammye Summers-Simmons
For editing, proof-reading and drawings she contributed.

My grandson, Chad L. Summers
For his graphic artwork and illustrations he contributed.

A very special friend Gloria White
For her expert proof reading.

And lastly to a very dear friend of the family, Sarah Baker
For her many drawings she contributed as well.

Contents

A Friendly Smile

There's nothing so contagious
As a friendly, winning smile
It travels on from face to face
And it gets brighter all the while.
It leaves a happy feeling
As it travels on its way
It lifts the hearts of many
Making them feel light and gay.
To ones deep in depression
Burdened with the cares of life
It provides a ray of sun shine
Hope of freedom the strife.
It makes the haughty heart grow kinder
When a smile lights up the face
And as it goes on, ever onward
It makes the world a better place.

Cumberland Dawn

As the day breaks o'er the mountain range
And the world begins to wake again
The sun peeps through the misty glow
The fog hangs heavy in clusters low
Between the hills, hiding valleys below.
Gone are the friends of the big old barn
That stands by the road in the early morn
And the road that twines around the hill
Never seems to be standing still
But travels on as the traveler will.
Such beautiful sight in the early morn
In the Cumberland hills where I was born,
Get up when the dew's still on the lawn
And follow the road to see a Cumberland dawn!

August Moon

The moon peeps over the mountain tall
And sends its beams down the long, green wall
To a valley small between the hills
Where a farmhouse stands lonely and still.
Its rays light up the goldenrod
Growing in the field beside the road
Their golden glow lovely to see
As the moon shines on them naturally.
As the moon climes higher into the sky
And the scene gets brighter by and by
The fence post look sentinels tall
Guarding the valley over all.
To enjoy this lovely scene
Wait 'til the moon peeps o'er the green
Then walk down the road
And not to soon
And enjoy a stroll ' neath
The August moon.

My Hollow

When darkness settles in my hollow in the hills
The night sounds give to me a thrill
Fire flies flittering moonbeams glittering
Down through the trees like birds on wing.
Crickets chirping in the bushes
Bullfrogs croaking in the rushes
The hoot of an owl in a far – off tree
The cry of a whip-poor-will close to me.
These are the sounds that I'll always hallow
Around my home up in the hollow.

Out of the Night

Out of the stillness of the night
Came the sound of the night bird's trill
It came through the window loud and clear
From the brow of the distant hill.
As I lay there and listened
To his melodious call
The answering trill came in on the wind
Faintly, barely heard at all.
'Twas a glorious thing of joy to hear
Such beauty out of sight
It made me know that God was there
In the stillness of the night.

Muses

When the sun goes down and skies are gray
O'er my mountain homestead far away
I sit and listen as the night bird sings
Then peace descends and spreads its wings
Like a dove on flight
Through the still dark night
I sit and think of my childhood days
The fun we had and the games we played
Down by the big old barn down by the brook
That rippled and laughed as we explored each nook
Those were the days that I liked best
And remember more than all the rest.

My Strength

The eastern hill where I was born
Have been strength to me
Strength to meet the cares of life
As they raced down life's troubled sea.
When I was young I roamed the hills
And sat in solitude by the mountain stream
And talked to God of many things
And bared my soul to him
Time was no element then
And as I sat I gathered strength alone
To tower above all of life's woes
And carry on to heights unknown.

The Hills of Old Kentucky

Is the place I want to be
Where the rhododendrons blossom
On the hill fair to see
And purest water trickles
Down the hill to make a stream
That flows down through the valley
Through the town and on again.
Where the wind is always blowing
Through the grove of stately pines
And the rain is so refreshing
In the good old summer time
And the people that you find there
Are as friendly as they can be
And they have a special way to show
Their mountain hospitality.
So 'way up in the mountains
Is the place I long to be
Where the air is always purest
In God's own country.

Signs of Spring

Breezes blowing through the trees
Waking up the birds and bees.
Buds bursting, sending out
Flowers, blooming all about.
Down in the meadow on a log
Sitting in the sun, old Grandfather Frog.
The blue bird singing a merry song
Spring is coming-it won't be long.

To Spring

The March wind blew across the land
And brought the April rain
It wet the earth and woke the flowers
And the grass turned green again.
Old Mother Crocus was first to wake
So she called to her little ones
'T is time to rise, hold your heads up high
To the rain and then the sun.
The birds returned, their warbles sweet
Trilled the air in the early morn
And then the trees put out their leaves
So the birds could build their homes.
It takes the wind and the gentle rain
To usher in the spring
And the sun to warm the cold, cold ground
To wake nature up again.

April

I took a stroll down a country lane
And saw the gentle April rain
Up on the grass and flowers and trees
And heard the humming of the bees.
The birds were as busy as could be
Building nest in every tree
Their music sweet filled the air
It made me glad that I was there.
I sat and rested on a stone
I was by myself, yet not alone
For God was there and I talked to Him
And thanked Him for the lovely spring.

The Wind

The wind is just a whispering breeze
It blows the trees and shakes the leaves
I feel it blowing through my hair
Its gentleness seems to fill the air
It blows the grasses at my feet
And makes the morning seems complete
It ruffles the feathers of a bird
Whose beautiful song I just heard
The beauty of the early morn
Envelopes me with all its charm
And I just sit and let it blow
And listen as it whispers low.

The Changing Seasons

When we see the time a-coming
And we know it want be long
'TIL it's time to dig the potatoes
And gather the corn
And the long, hot day of summer
Will soon be o'er and gone
Then we can think about autumn
And the breezy days to come.
When the sun's a little hazy
And sets blood-red in the west
And warms the cool autumn winds
As they blow across the earth's breast
And we see the autumn colors
In their splendor start to glow
Then we can forget about the autumn
And begin to think about the snow.
When the days start growing colder
And the winds begin to blow
And we know that the winter
Will soon usher in the snow
And the wondrous scenes of winter time
Put on a silvery glow

Then we can think about the spring time
And the lovely things that grow.
When we see the lovely seasons
Going by us one by one
And we watch the sun a-setting
On each lovely scene undone.
And no matter what the seasons
That is passing by us fair
Then we can look up to our Maker
And we can know that He is there.

In the Autumn

I like to go down a country land
A see the fields of golden grain
Being harvested 'fore the autumn rain
And beyond the fields of corn
Where the baby pumpkins all were born
Now they are huge, round balls waiting for
Cinderella's call-
Or, just for dinner, a pumpkin pie
The sight of which lights up the eye
Around the bend the orchard stands
With rolls of trees on every hand
The apples round, all red and yellow
Waiting to get a little mellow
Before they let go of the tree
This is a beautiful thing to see.
Down the country lane in fall
Is the most wonderful sight of all.

When Seasons Change

When summer's green turn to autumn's gold
And the winter's days come very cold
And the north winds blow across the way
Bringing ice and snow to stay
We have a different world, quite
With snow falling through the night
To make a fairyland of white
More beautiful than artist's pen
Can paint on canvas ever then
And we can look out and behold our land
This lovely scene made not by man
Such beauty rare at God's hand.
When we see these changing times
With control of any clime
We know there is a Power Divine
Watching o'er us all the time

Ready For Winter

The golden rod is yellow
And it's blooming every where
The cat tails in the march
Reaching high into the air
The hickory nuts are falling
And it's time to gather in
The fruits ripe from the summer
Safely stack within the bin
For we can tell by tell by the weather
That old winter's on its way
And we know we must be ready
For that icy, wintry day.
And with the changing season
Comes the loveliest scene of all
When the trees are decorated
With bright colors of the fall
Then the winds begin to blowing
And the birds leave for the south
And the squirrel running to and fro
With walnuts in his mouth
Preparing for the cold winter
Days which are a head

When he can curl up and sleep warmly
In his cozy little bed.
So, one and all get ready
For the time is coming fast
When the trees will lose their glory
And the autumn days will pass
When the harvest time is over
And the wood is in the bin
And the north wind blows around the house
Trying so hard to get in
Then we can sit beside the fire
In our cozy room abide
And never have to worry about
The goings on outside.

O Rainy Day

O rainy day in fall
Most dismal time of all
Your icy touch
Is just too much
You usher in October's chill
We must accept against our will
Never ready for this time of year
Even though we know it's near.
You bring to us the last season
For a very special reason
For we know that Nature has to rest
To get ready for the time that's best
When she begins to sprout and grow
And bring to us the spring-like glow
Of green upon our barren land
We know that spring is close at hand.
So come what may
O rainy day
We will accept your chill
And colder days at your will
But remember all of this will pass
And spring we know will come at last
And bring to us another clime
Worth waiting for with its joy sublime.

Jack Frost

Old Jack Frost is a merry little elf
He uses the branch of the tree for a shelf
And with brush in hand he paints the leaves
Red, Brown and yellow on the trees
But when he gets to the windowpanes
He etches pictures with icicle canes
He makes fairy castles and mountains high
That sparkle and shining against the sky
He touches the grasses here and there
And diamonds sparkle everywhere
When each fencepost wears a cap of white
His work is finished for the night
And with a satisfied, impish smile
He runs away to rest awhile.

Halloween

When October days come to an end
'Tis time for witches to come again
Bring with them old black cats
Riding on broomsticks in tall black hats.
They fly around in the light of the moon
With black cats hanging on to the brooms
And black bats flying round and round
As they circle around the town.
The ghouls and goblins are all about
To scare you when you venture out
To see the Jack-o-lanterns bright
Glowing fire into the night.
And don't forget, there's ghosts about
To jump at you and make you shout
Their eerie sounds fill the air
Seems like they are everywhere
So don't get caught out in the dark
Unless you have a light to spark
To help keep ghosts away from you
And scare the ghouls and goblins too!

Snow Magic

The snow fairy came in the dark of the night
And made a cover of snowy white
Dressing all the evergreen trees
With lacy gowns all silvery.
The tall black trees stand bleak and bare
Spreading their branches into the air
With a most majestic flair
Shivering in the frosty air.
Each roof-top has a blanket white
To keep the house warm through the night
And every fencepost in the row
Wears a puffy hat of snow
No tracks left on the snowy lawn
As morning breaks at
Early dawn
God's beauty not yet marred by man
Is spread in splendor o'er the land.

No Room

No room in the inn for the the travelers at all
No place for them but a stable small
There the Saviour was born
In the cold, cold night
By the light of the star that shone so bright.
Had the innkeeper known whom he turned away
He would have made room
For them to stay
In the inn instead of the stable so low
But the good news wasn't
For him to know.
The shepherds in the fields that night
Saw the light shine forth with all its might
Then the angels told the news to them
And they came to the stable to worship Him.
The Wise men traveled from afar
They made their way, led by the star
To Bethlehem where the
Christ Child was born
On that wonderful wintry morn.

When the Saviour Came

The bells rang out in the
Still dark night
The animals kneeled at
The lovely sight
The star shone bright
With a radiant glow
The angels sang so sweet and low
When the Saviour came
To the earth below.
And each year when the
Bells ring true
Spreading love and joy
The whole year through
Let's not forget that
On that night
He came to save us
From our plight
While angels sang
In the still dark night.

Bells of Christmas

Hear the joy bells
Ringing clear
Through the frosty
Morning air
Bells of Christmas
Hear them chime
Reminding us it's
Christmas time.
Time to spread a
Little cheer
That will last throughout
The year
Bells of Christmas, hear
Them ring
Telling all the world
To sing.
Bells of Christmas ring
Loud and clear
Through the frosty
Morning air
'Tis the birthday of
Our King
That's why Christmas bells
Must ring.

Ring Out The Old

The year is quickly passing by
As we look back when it began
It seem but only yesterday when
The old man left and the baby came.
Ring out the old,
Ring in the new
And hope for better days to come
And let us make the best of them
'Ere like the old year
They are gone.
Let our resolutions always be
To do good things each day we live
And depend on God to see us through
Then to us He will His
Blessings give.
So, ring out the old, ring in the new
And hope for better days to come
And let us make the best of them
'Ere like the old year
They are gone.

Winters Fling

Old man winter is having a fling
Trying to hinder the entrance of spring
The snow has lost its sparkling glow
And is old and dirty and full of holes
The earth is tired of lying low
And is eager to break forth and grow
But winter keeps on hanging on
Sending its blast to stop the song
Of the birds here to herald spring
Nipping the bud of each living thing
Soon it will have to end its fling
And make way for the glorious spring.

O Spring

Break forth, O Spring, in all
Your splendor
And take away the ravages
Of winter
Shower us with your lovely green
And gentle breezes and April rain
Bring back the birds from
Far –off places
And let the sun shine
On our faces
We're tired of winter and
The cold
It makes us feel we're
Getting old
O Spring, awake and bring again
To us who wait your lovely scene.

Gods World

I like to get up early in the morning
And watch the world wake up
God's world to me
The natural things around us
Most people seldom see.
This morning I saw a cardinal
In his bright coat of red
Then came a robin redbreast
Proudly holding up his head.
A red-winged blackbird took a bath
In the little stream behind my house
And sat on the grapevine in the sun
Preening his feathers, one by one.
Now and then a mockingbird
Makes his presence known
And cheers the world around him
By sending forth his lovely song.
Little by little the green leaves
And the jonquils and the daffodils
Are waving and nodding in the breeze.
Such a lovely morning
God has given me
That's why I get up early
His beautiful world to see.

Night Magic

When the shadows steal across the grass
And the sun is gone from the western sky
The keepers of the day must rest
And bid the world good-by.
As the darkness of the night sets in
And everything is still
The creatures of the night awake
To the cry of the whip-poor-will.
The night owl sits in an old oak tree
Watching the magic of the night
And winks his eye as the firefly
Flits around and shines his light.
Down through the leaves of the old oak tree
The pale moon sends its silvery glow
To shine on the back of an old raccoon
Lighting the way for him to go.
So on goes the magic of the night
As time creeps toward the dawn of day
The old owl gives a sudden hoot-
And the night creatures begin to scamper away.

The Storm

The rain came down in sheets today
And splashed against the window pane
The thunder rolled across the way
And the lighting streaked as if insane.
The wind blew hard against the trees
Blending them low from side to side
The air was full of fluttering leaves
Trying to find a place to hide.
The hailstones beat against the glass
Striking up a lively tune
And while the storm was raging past
I was safe and sound in my cozy room.

I Wonder

The world goes by and
I stand still
And watch from my place
Up the hill
I see the hurrying
Of many feet
As they rush along
The busy street
Never taking time to
Stop and say
Hello, or how are
You today
Too busy to enjoy
Their life
All thoughts of fun lost
In the strife
And even God is
Put aside
Lost in the rush of
The maddening tide
And worldly cares come
Rushing in

To take their minds
Away from Him.
As I watch all of this
From my hill
I wonder if they
Ever will
From the worldly
Turn away
And take the time
To stop and say
A kind word to a
Soul in need
Or the hungry ones
Help to feed
And make some friends
Along the way
And take some time
Alone to pray
For God to help them
In their quest To find the joys
Of happiness.

Self- Righteousness

When a man has a mind of his own
And he thinks his way is the best
Sometimes, when tried, his way proves wrong
When it is put to the test.
His way is never wrong to him
There is always a reason why
His way didn't turn out all right
And he buffs it off with a sigh.
This type of man has a narrow mind
When only his way will do
But the man who can see beyond his way
Will see good in others, too.
The man who sees his way as best
Will be a lonely man
For others will stay away from him
And leave him to his plan.
And when he sees, ' twill be too late
That his way's not the only one
He'll find it hard to make new friends
Because of the things he's done.
So don't be like the narrow mind
But reach out to others strong
And you will be liked by others too
And missed when you are gone.

Which Way?

Our life is but a short span
Of time on earth we know
And what we do while we are here
Is a choice we make also.
There are two roads we can take
We choose the one we may
One is a broad and easy road
A deceptive, sinful way.
The other road is narrow and straight
And hard to travel on
But if we choose to take this road
We'll find it won't be wrong.
The broad road leads us far away
From Heaven's open door
To the gates of Hell where Satan reigns
To be lost forever more.
So let's get on the narrow road
And from it never roam
Because we know at the end of it
We'll find a blessed home.

The Last Walk

When I have reached the
Bend in the road
And you've gone as far as
You can with me.
Don't hesitate to let me go
For I have a Friend
Whose face I'll see
That will take my hand
And lead me on
Through the valley beyond
And to my home
Together we'll walk
Through Heaven's door
And abide in peace
Forever more.

In Memory Of

Little hands-oh what a joy
To feel them warm and sweet
A little body cuddling close
The patter of little feet.
I hear the clanking of a wagon
The bouncing of a ball
But when I go to find the noise
I can't find the place at all.
A jolt-and I'm myself again
That was one year ago
When our little boy was with us
We worshiped him, you know.
Jesus came to visit us
And took our little lad
And with him went our happiness
And left our home so sad,
Tonight –a little angel
Looks down on us below
And sees his father and mother
And the Ma that loved him so.
"1937"

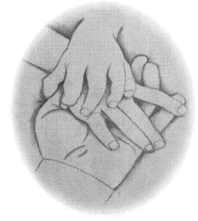

To My Children

When from this world I've departed
Leaving all my loved ones behind
May they not be down-hearted
May they have peace of mind.
Although they may feel lonely
A vacant place to see
May they not grieve, but only
May they still remember me.
The happiness they brought
The laughter light and gay
The many things I taught
To them day after day
To me they were my jewels
Bright shining precious gems
That filled my life with sunshine
For this He sent me them.
So may they not be lonely
May they not be sad and blue
May they remember only
That I loved them true.

May they remember the joy they brought me
All the happiness and love
May they know that I am happy
In my home in Heaven above.
May they ever look to Jesus
Walk the straight and narrow way
And with the help of our dear Saviour
We will meet again someday.

To My Husband

If I could turn back through the years
And begin again the upward climb
I'd want you by my side, my own
Always your hand in mine.
The many things we have shared
Have drawn us closer, dear
No matter how rough, the way
Seemed smoother with you near.
And in the times of deepest stress
When I was sad and blue
You were there to comfort me
With your love so true.
I would not change one moment
One hour, year or day
Of time with you, my dearest one
You're in my heart to stay.
What happens in the future
Can never change the past
As long as I shall live, my dear
My love for you will last.

In Remembrance

The little school has closed at last
The children have gone home
It's sad to think the time has passed
And I sit here alone.
Traveling down memory lane
My thoughts begin to soar
And take me back to yesterday
And Mallie School once more.
To children and their laughter gay
Their problems and their tears
That I have helped along the way
These twenty happy years.
Happy voices raised in singing
Songs so light and gay
Then in silence, lessons getting
To recite, so they could play.
Many little lives I've guided
Ever onward toward their goal
Teaching them the finer things
From which their lives to mold.

As they travel ever onward
May they keep on looking up
May their footsteps never falter
Until they have reached the top.
May each one have caught a vision
May each one be always true
Look to God for help and guidance
Reach his goal and carry through.

A Grave or A Rut

A rut can be a small thing
Dug out by driving rain
Washing down a gully
Or perhaps across a plain.
It can be deepened or made wider
By a car or wagon, but
However it happened
It is still only a rut.
A grave is a different thing
It can be large or small
A certain width and length, but depth
Is six feet-that is all.
What is the significance of a grave
To hold some one most dear
Only the body's resting place
'Til the end of time is near.
The difference between a grave and a rut
Is length and width and height
The grave-significance
The rut-a sorry sight.

Sea Phantom

The mist hung low o'er the sea
Veiling sight and muffling sound
The fog horn sounded dismally
As on the surf the waves did pound.
He sat alone beside the sea
The pounding waves beat high
The tide came in, the mist grew thick
He listened-heard the winds sigh.
Too often had he come to this
Waiting, listening as sea did reign
Not caring how the sea came in
But that she should come in again.
He saw her as she tripped along
Toward him in the thickening gloom
She passed him by as though a ghost
Would tread the shores unknown.
"Come back, tis I!" his lovely cry
Resounded on the shore
She vanished in the deepening mist
He was alone once more.

The Sea And I

I like to go down by the sea
And sit alone on the sandy shore
And watch the waves as they come in
Pounding from the ocean floor
I am no stranger to the sea
And as it rolls in, it speaks to me
And tells me of strange, far off lands
And places I would like to see.
'Tis' sweet music to my ears
The nearing of the ocean wave
And I could stay a thousand years
And let it wash upon my grave.
So, Mighty Sea, keep dashing high
Upon the bleak and lonely shore
And even though in my grave I lie
I can hear you pound from the ocean floor.

Retirement

Don't let retirement be
A time of discontent
But use the time in such a way
That it will be well spent.
And do not wait until too old
Retire as soon as you can
Enjoy the pleasures that life holds
Be your own woman or man.
So don't let retirement be
A time of sorrow a d discontent
But do the things you like to do
And it will be time well spent.

Retirement

Retirement is what you make it
It can be a time of sadness and lament
Or it can be a time happy and gay
But you're the one to choose the way.
If you face it with a smile
You will be happy all the while
Each day will as a moment be
With so many things to do and see.
So take a little time each day
To read God's word and pray
And you will find you will be blessed
And you'll reap the joys of happiness.
Then retirement will fulfill for you
The dreams you've had your life-long through
And by doing the things you like to do
Make retirement mean the most to you.

On Marriage

May your marriage be
As the rising sun
Full of warmth and love
Togetherness as one.
Sometimes when things go wrong
And both are much displeased
Think of the vows you made
'twill put your mind at ease.
If a marriage is built on truth
And the wonderfulness of love
Nothing can break the ties
That binds it from above.
Don't let your love grow old
Forever keep it young
And you will greet each day
As bright as the morning sun.
Always rely on God
To help in times of stress
And your lives will be filled
With love and happiness.

Marriage

Marriage is a union
And it can be made happy
By God's blessing from above,
Each one must give and take
And turn to God each day
For wisdom and strength
To guide in every way.
Vows taken on that wonderful day
Must be kept sacred by both, you know
And as you live from day to day
Marriage will dearer and dearer grow.

Love

Love is like a rose
It blooms and grows
And sheds its beauty
For a while.
Then evil thoughts come in
To mar its beauty
And breaks the bonds
That ties two people together
Love must not fade
If it is to last forever
Evil thoughts must be over come
With thoughts of love so strong
That they will hold together
The bonds of love
Between two people forever.

I Miss You

I miss you in the early morn
When the grass is wet with dew
I miss you every moment, dear
That I am not with you
I miss you in the twilight time
When the evening breezes blow
And I am in the garden
Where the little fire flies glow.
I wonder if you miss me too
When you are far away

And if you long to see me
Enough to hurry back one day.
You know I love you dearly
And want to be with you
And long to hear you say again
That you also love me true.
I long to see the time pass by
And soon we'll be as one
Our love will span the bridge of time
'till the setting of the sun.

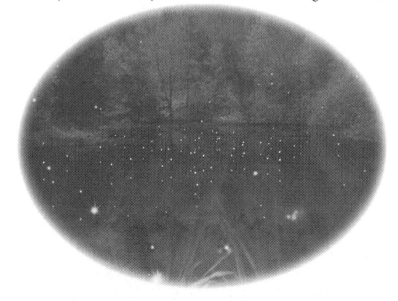

My Love

My love is like a red rose fair
With laughing eyes and curly hair
And a gentle smile upon her face
Her every movement full of grace.
She always knows just what to do
When I am sad or when I'm blue
Her love for me will always shine
And last until the end of time.

Our Life Together

Time is swiftly passing by
Looking back when our love began
It seems 'twas only yesterday
When first you held my hand.
Hand in hand we've walked together
Shared our laughter and our tears
Our love has been a wonderful venture
As we've journeyed together through the years.
And so as time goes marching on
We'll face our joys and sorrows
The bond of love will hold us strong
And last through our tomorrows.

Our Love

As we sit beside the fire
With the embers burning low
We're thinking of the days gone by
And our love pact of long ago.
Then our love, like the new-made fire
Burned with a passionate glow
And it lasted through the years
A love that is wonderful to know.
Now with the slowly burning embers
Casting shadows, his and mine
Show our love still stands undaunted
By the ravages of time.
(On our 45th anniversary)

If

If someday the time should come
That you and I should part
Even though I know you're gone
You'll still live in my heart.
I'll still have all my memories
Sweet, that will always linger on
I'll try not to face reality
And the fact that you are gone.
But while we're still together
And until death do us part
Let's let our love for each other
Reign uppermost in our hearts.

Our Fifty Years

When shadows fall and day is done
And stars light up the sky
I sit alone and think of you
And happy days gone by.
We strolled beneath the silvery moon
And wished on every star
That our love would throughout the years
That together we'd travel far.
And then upon our wedding day
We made our vows so true.
To love and cherish 'til death should part
As we were meant to do.
Down through time we've kept our vows
And until this very day
Our love has blossomed like a flower
And will never fade away.
Together we've shared much happiness
And with stood our sorrows too
The love we found when we were young
Became the bond that brought us through.
Now as we face the future
Until the very end
We'll travel on from day to day
Together, hand in hand.

April Rain

What is more refreshing
Than a dash of April rain?
It kisses all the flowers
And makes the grass turn green
It gives the good old earth a bath
And makes it look so clean-
There's nothing so refreshing
As a dash of April rain.
It call the leaves to open up
And dress up all the trees
And to open up their blossoms
For the busy little bees
It washes down the rooftops
And dots the window panes
There's nothing so refreshing
As a dash of April rain.
And with the dash of April rain
The gentle breeze blow
They help the rain to clean the earth
And help God's garden grow.
Then for a while the sun comes out
And dries the earth again
There's nothing more refreshing
Than God's whole nature plan.

August Sunset

The sun set red far in the west
From where I sat I could behold
The waters on the rippling lake
Splashed with the colors, red and gold.
I sat and watched the shimmering scene
'til it faded slowly into grey
The sun dipped down behind the trees
Bringing to a close, the day.
The beauty of this wondrous scene
Cannot be caught by poets' pens
Nor will the colors be the same
When they are caught by the cameras lens.
Such loveliness only portrayed by God
As I sat there in reverent awe
I tried to imprint upon my mind
The lovely sunset that I saw.
Each evening after that I watched
The sunset down behind the trees
But never did it look the same
As it did that day on the rippling sea.

Be Thankful

Be Thankful for the little things
That happen day by day
For food we eat, the clothes we wear
For time to work and play.
Be thankful for the strength we have
To do each little chore
And health to live and work and play
For these and many more
Be thankful for a time of rest
To read and think and pray
Be thankful for the setting sun
The ending of each day.
Be thankful for our children dear
And for our friends around us
And for the Father up above
In whom we put our trust.
So on this new Thanksgiving Day
Let's not forget gifts, large or small
Let's bow our heads in humbleness
And thank our Father for them all.

Thanksgiving

Thanksgiving is a special time
We have to spend together
To be thankful for the things we have
Regardless of the weather.
It's also time to greet our friends
And send them wishes true
That God may touch them with his love
Bring them joy and happiness too.
Now as we gather 'round the table
Seeing such a food array
Let us thank our Heavenly Father
For this, our Thanksgiving Day.

Twilight Time

When day is done and shadows fall
And the sun sets in the west
And twilight time is ushered in
The time of day that's best
I sit and watch the darkness fall
And see the fireflies glow
They look just like a million stars
Twinkling to and fro.
The birds have gone to their hiding place
To rest till the break of morn
The hum-drum noise of the day time
Has lulled like a mighty storm.
And so I sit quietly
And let my thoughts stray afar
'til darkness falls upon the land
And I behold the Evening Star.
Night sets in and breaks the spell
The magic moments are gone too soon
The sky lights with twinkling stars
Making way for the round, full moon.
Night time brings its magic too
With twinkling stars and bright moonshine
But the time between the day and night
Is the best for me-it's twilight time.

Meditation

Oh, to walk through the meadow
When the dew is wet
To reach down to pick
A blue violet
To hear the drone of a
Bee close by
Catch a glimpse of
A rabbit
From the corner of
My eye
To feel the cool breeze
Of the early morn
Hear the tinkle of the cowbell
As she shakes her horn
To listen to the tune of
The babbling brook
Winding and laughing
With every little crook
To hear the beautiful meadowlark
Singing its song
To be by myself just walking alone
In the quiet of the meadow in the early dawn!

The Sudden Storm

The clouds looked angry,
Heading southward on
Its way
The sun replaced the
Raging storm
And made a perfect ending
For the day
black and gray
As the storm moved in above the town
The lighting, streaking
on its way
Parted the clouds and the rain poured down.
The thunder roared and
seemed a-flame
As the lighting flashed and
the storm raged on
The hailstones beat the
window panes
The fierce winds blew
the storm along.
It left as quickly as
it was borne.

T-Ball

Of all the sports there are to see
T-Ball is the game for me
As you watch each batter up to bat
Each little boy in his red hard-hat.
He swings his bat just like the pros
And imitates someone he knows
And then he runs with all his might
And makes a slide to the base-all right!
When the time is right and he steals base
A great big smile spreads over his face
And he looks around as if to say
"we're going to win this game today!"
If you've never been to a T-Ball game
You've no one but yourself to blame
So go to the ball park, one and all
And see the best game in sports-T-Ball.

In Kentucky

It's great to be a wildcat fan
Just take a look at what's running around
In Kentucky
There's a goose on the loose
That puts the ball through with a swoosh
In Kentucky
There's a man that can cram
And can't be stopped when he's on the lam
In Kentucky
There's a man that can bomb

No matter where it's from
In Kentucky
There's a man, when fouled, puts on a show
And hardly ever misses a free throw
In Kentucky.
He brings up the ball and calls the play
And goes to the hoop, and that's all.
In Kentucky
There's a man full of wit
That can grab that ball and dribble it

In Kentucky
Then there's a bench strong and tall
That can come in and handle the ball
In Kentucky
Behind all this there's a couch
That no other can approach
In Kentucky
Now you can see just what we mean
When we say we've got the Champion Team
In Kentucky!

Bells

Bells ring out all
Through the year
With many a different
Meaning
But the bells that I
Most like to hear
Are the happy school
Bells ringing.

My Prayer

If I have done one thing today
To cause someone to go astray
Forgive me, Lord is my humble prayer
I pray to you in this dark hour.
Lift me up and hold my hand
Help me, I pray, to understand
The wrong I've done to my fellowman.
Give me the words to right the wrong
Put in my heart a happy song
To sing to others of your love
And your watchful eyes from up above
To show them how to live for thee
As they travel on life's sea.
Grant, Oh Lord, this prayer from me.

Hills And Valleys

If you can count the hills and valleys
As you go along life's way-
The times upon the mountain top
When life seems bright and gay-
The times down in the valley
That are filled with dark despair,
And you forget to count your blessings
Whether you're low or in the air-
Then you will miss your calling
As you travel on your way
You will not realize God's blessings"
Or his care for you each day
When you are you at the highest point
Thank God for being there
And when you're at the lowest ebb
You'll know that He still cares.
Then let Him lead you to the highest hill
When your life is light and gay
And He'll take your hand and lead you
Through the valleys on the way.

The Fragrance Of The Rose

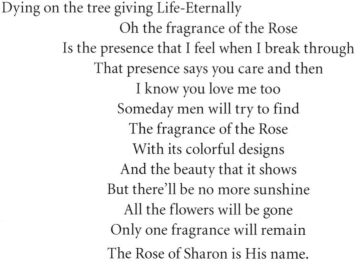

Just picture a Rose
With it's colorful design
And smell the fragrance of a Rose
In the morning's bright sunshine
Just picture the Rose
Hanging there upon the tree
And smell the fragrance of the Rose
As HE dies so willingly
Oh the fragrance of the Rose
As he dies so willingly
Oh the fragrance of the Rose
Is like no other fragrance in the world
It's being crushed for me unselfishly
Dying on the tree giving Life-Eternally
Oh the fragrance of the Rose
Is the presence that I feel when I break through
That presence says you care and then
I know you love me too
Someday men will try to find
The fragrance of the Rose
With its colorful designs
And the beauty that it shows
But there'll be no more sunshine
All the flowers will be gone
Only one fragrance will remain
The Rose of Sharon is His name.

The Saviour

God sent His son to earth one day
To save us all from sin
And when He knocks on our heart's door
We must open it and let Him in.
He wasn't here for very long
But He had so much to do
He healed the sick, made the blind to see
And cleansed the lepers, too.
He went about from place to place
His miracles to perform
The people even climbed the trees
He was their shelter from the storm.
He told the disciples that He must go
To prepare a place for them
And they must carry on His work
They could not go with Him.
Then they all cried out to Him
They wanted Him to stay
But Judas betrayed Him that very night
For a very little pay.
They took Him to the mountaintop
And nailed Him to the cross

The disciples looked on helplessly
They could hardly bear their loss.
They laid Him in a new-made tomb
A boulder sealed the door
But in three days it was rolled away
And our Lord was there no more.
Now He reigns with God above
Where He's preparing a new home
For all who love and follow Him
And live for Him alone.
So we must be ready when He knocks
And open up the door
Then when he comes, we'll be with Him
And live forever more.